the zen of
wilderness and walking
wit, wisdom, and inspiration

foreword by Bill McKibben

edited by Katharine Wroth
illustrations by Kate Quinby

SKIPSTONE

Published by Skipstone, an imprint of The Mountaineers Books
Manufactured in the United States of America

First printing 2009
12 11 10 09   5 4 3 2 1

Compiled and edited by Katherine Wroth
Illustrations by Kate Quinby
Design by Heidi Smets
Cover photograph from stock.xchange

ISBN 978-1-59485-107-0

Library of Congress Cataloging-in-Publication Data
The zen of wilderness and walking : wit, wisdom, and inspiration / foreword by Bill McKibben ; edited by Katharine Wroth ; illustrations by Kate Quinby.
    p. cm.
Includes bibliographical references and index.
ISBN-13: 978-1-59485-107-0 (alk. paper)
ISBN-10: 1-59485-107-7 (alk. paper)
1. Wilderness areas—Quotations, maxims, etc. 2. Walking—Quotations, maxims, etc. I. Wroth, Katharine. II. Quinby, Kate, ill.
PN6084.W47Z46 2009
796.51—dc22
                    2008048787

Skipstone books may be purchased for corporate, educational, or other promotional sales. For special discounts and information, contact our Sales Department at 800-553-4453 or mbooks@mountaineersbooks.org.

Skipstone
1001 SW Klickitat Way, Suite 201
Seattle, Washington 98134
206.223.6303
www.skipstonepress.org
www.mountaineersbooks.org

FIBER USED IN THIS PRODUCT LINE MEETS THE SOURCING REQUIREMENTS OF THE SFI PROGRAM
WWW.SFIPROGRAM.ORG

LIVE LIFE. MAKE RIPPLES.

Now I see the secret of the making of the best persons,
It is to grow in the open air and to eat and sleep with
the earth.

—Walt Whitman

walk with me

by Bill McKibben

Confession: I spend an enormous amount of my life in airplanes. It's a sin—my carbon footprint is more like a tank tread—but since all of the travel is devoted to fighting global warming, I somehow manage to deal with the hypocrisy. But I can't deal with the sitting on my butt. It is absolute dead time, to be endured: newspapers, books, DVDs, anything to kill the soulless monotony of my cramped little cage. The very opposite of taking a walk.

I live in the woods, and so can be swallowed up in the forest ten steps out my back door. Swallowed up, that is, in the astonishing richness of the out-of-doors. Sights: the fleeting glimpse of a fleeing fox, the deep leathery green of an August leaf, the sun drifting through the gaps in the canopy. Smells: the subtly overpowering scent of rain, my very favorite. Sounds: the stream growing louder, the tops of the hemlocks swaying in the breeze. The feel of that breeze against my forearms. (Once I stepped on a yellow jacket nest—now that is feeling.)

If I walk for an hour, I travel farther than if I fly for six. I travel deep into the moment.

And if I go for more than an hour? Then it really gets good.

A few years ago, just sick to death of travel, I took my vacation out the back door. I hoisted a pack on my back and walked for three weeks. Some of it was on mountain trail, and some of it was on the shoulder of county road, and all of it was glorious, especially as I sank into the rhythm, as the chatter of my internal CNN began to die down. You see things differently on foot, of course: the rise that goes unnoticed in the car, that can cause you to depress the angle of your ankle a degree or two, is immediately obvious. And friends welcome you differently when you arrive on foot: they know you're not breezing in for an hour and then heading back home. You're a sojourner. They know you'll really be visiting.

A year or two after that long walk, I organized a very different sort of hike. This one lasted five days and spanned my corner of Vermont. It was designed to call attention to global warming, and hence it required large numbers of participants. By its end there were a thousand people marching, which in Vermont is an enormous number. A loner at heart, I'd worried that hiking with so many others would be irksome, but just the opposite proved to be the case. You had ten hours on foot a day, so there was no need to "cut to the chase" or "make a long story short." You really got to know the people you walked beside. The rhythm of walking became the rhythm of fellowship.

The quotations collected here give a nod to that sense of fellowship—as well as the many other joys to be found when one leaves cars and planes and trains behind. They remind us why it is not only pleasant—but absolutely necessary—to set out on foot on occasion. And I'll add one more quotation to the pile; it comes from Thoreau, who was not only our greatest philosopher, but (and they are clearly linked) our greatest walker. "I think that I cannot preserve my health and spirits, unless I spend four hours a day at least—and it is commonly more than that—sauntering through the woods and over the hills and fields, absolutely free from all worldly engagements."

I agree, which is why I'm going crazy here at the keyboard. Time for a walk.

the woods and wilds we explore

Whether they are on a brief ramble through the back forty or a multiday trek in the mountains, those on foot find inspiration in the flowers, trees, and hills they encounter.

When we walk, we naturally go to the fields and woods: what would become of us, if we walked only in a garden or a mall?

—Henry David Thoreau

Thousands of tired, nerve-shaken, over-civilized people are beginning to find out that going to the mountains is going home; that wildness is a necessity; and that mountain parks and reservations are useful not only as fountains of timber and irrigating rivers, but as fountains of life.

—John Muir

What a joy it is to feel the soft, springy earth under my feet once more, to follow grassy roads that lead to ferny brooks where I can bathe my fingers in a cataract of rippling notes, or to clamber over a stone wall into green fields that tumble and roll and climb in riotous gladness!

—Helen Keller

Everybody who's anybody longs to be a tree—

—Rita Dove

The pine tree seems to listen, the fir tree seems to wait, and neither with impatience: they give no thought to the little people below them whose impatience and curiosity eat them up alive.

—Friedrich Nietzsche

To a person uninstructed in natural history, his country or sea-side stroll is a walk through a gallery filled with wonderful works of art, nine-tenths of which have their faces turned to the wall. Teach him something of natural history, and you place in his hands a catalogue of those which are worth turning round.

—Thomas Henry Huxley

I think it pisses God off if you walk by the color purple in a field somewhere and don't notice it.

—Alice Walker

The benefit of out-of-doors is not that it takes us away from civilization, but that it restores us to ourselves. Its profound essential satisfactions build themselves into the character and become part of the personality.

—Bliss Carman

One weakness in our appreciation of nature is the emphasis placed upon *scenery*, which in its exploited aspect is merely a gargantuan curio. Things are appreciated for size, unusuality, and scarcity more than for their subtleties and emotional relationship to everyday life.

—Ansel Adams

A single fiber does not make a thread, nor a single tree a forest.

The tree which moves some to tears of joy is in the eyes of others only a green thing that stands in the way. Some see nature all ridicule and deformity … and some scarce see nature at all. But to the eyes of the man of imagination, nature is imagination itself.

—William Blake

I believe in evolution. But I also believe, when I hike the Grand Canyon and see it at sunset, that the hand of God is there also.

—John McCain

Growing up in the Bay Area, I relished occasional car trips into the vastness and beauty of the Sierra Nevada. But as a householder in Vermont, I love even more the tattered, recovering wilderness just outside our back door, where in every season our family can ramble among the crags that overhang our roof and that frame the playing fields of the children's schools.

—John Elder

I am savage enough to prefer the woods, the wilds, and the independence of Monticello, to all the brilliant pleasures of this gay capital.

—Thomas Jefferson, on Paris

I have need of the sky,
I have business with the grass;
I will up and get me away where the hawk is wheeling
Lone and high,
And the slow clouds go by.
I will get me away to the waters that glass
The clouds as they pass.
I will get me away to the woods.

—Richard Hovey

Wilderness … functions as the other of culture. It is a place that we can visit, but we do not belong there.

—Jonathan Maskit

No one can walk in a road cut through pine woods without being struck by the architectural appearance of the grove, especially in winter when the bareness of the trees shows the low arch of the Saxons. In the woods in a winter afternoon one will see as readily the origin of the stained glass window … in the colors of the western sky seen through the bare and crossing branches of the forest.

—Ralph Waldo Emerson

We must not always talk in the market-place of what happens to us in the forest.

—Nathaniel Hawthorne

Be scared. You can't help that. But don't be afraid. Ain't nothing in the woods going to hurt you unless you corner it, or it smells that you are afraid. A bear or a deer, too, has got to be scared of a coward the same as a brave man has got to be.

—William Faulkner

I like big, open, spare landscapes. There's lots of room.
Nobody bothers you … I feel as if I can think there.

—Gretel Ehrlich

In the desert, I hoped to find pure nature, in its canyons the keys to mysteries, on its peaks perhaps even transcendence.

—Lawrence Hogue

When you take a flower in your hand and really look at it,
it's your world for the moment.

—Georgia O'Keeffe

All my life through, the new sights of nature made me
rejoice like a child.

—Marie Curie

Not to find one's way in a city may well be uninteresting and banal. It requires ignorance—nothing more. But to lose oneself in a city—as one loses oneself in a forest—that calls for a quite different schooling. Then, signboard and street names, passers-by, roofs, kiosks, or bars must speak to the wanderer like a cracking twig under his feet in the forest.

—Walter Benjamin

You linger your little hour and are gone,
And still the woods sweep leafily on,

—Robert Frost

on the move

Lace up your boots, organize your pack, sling it on your back, and off you go! You know the drill, and you know just how good it feels to put one foot in front of the other.

Taste your legs, sir: put them to motion.

—Shakespeare (*Twelfth Night*)

To my surprise, I felt a certain springy keenness. I was ready to hike. I had waited months for this day, after all, even if it had been mostly with foreboding. I wanted to see what was out there. All over America today people would be dragging themselves to work, stuck in traffic jams, wreathed in exhaust smoke. I was going for a walk in the woods.

—Bill Bryson

When the sun's behind the mountain and the frost is
in the air,
We're up and off and hiking on our way;
We don't know where we're going and we don't
supremely care,
But we'll be there when the evening ends the day.

—Sierra Club song

My pack weighs about twenty pounds. We are light of step and light of heart … What a blessing it is to be alive, and to be hiking again in the wilderness.

—Amy Racina

The stronger you make your body and the lighter you make your pack, the more upright you'll hike and the more you'll enjoy the scenery you came to see.

—FLAB: Fun-Loving, Adventuresome Broads

Figured I'd go out and go for a walk.
[My girlfriend] said, "How long are you going to be gone?"
I said, "The whole time."

—Stephen Wright

I'm a hiking boots woman.
I've gotta get moving along.

—Martha Haehl

My grandmother started walking five miles a day when she was sixty. She's ninety-seven today. We don't know where the hell she is.

—Ellen DeGeneres

I'm so happy just walking along a creek and seeing how it all changes every day.

—Gretel Ehrlich

If I could not walk far and fast, I think I should just explode and perish.

—Charles Dickens

When walking, walk. When eating, eat.

—Zen proverb

The only hike I ever took was when my grandpa told me to get outta his sight when I was being too loud. I'd hike my butt out of that room real quick.

—Johnny Tapia

Almost all backcountry woes can be traced to one simple cause: Trying to go too far too fast too high too soon.

—Karen Berger

Dear Lord, if you pick 'em up, I'll put 'em down.

—Hiker's Prayer

Why not walk in the aura of magic that gives to the small things of life their uniqueness and importance? Why not befriend a toad today?

—Germaine Greer

Certainly my own most memorable hikes can be classified as Shortcuts that Backfired.

—Edward Abbey

The man with the knapsack is never lost. No matter whither he may stray, his food and shelter are right with him, and home is wherever he may choose to stop.

—Horace Kephart

Trail travel expects self-reliance. If you don't do your own housekeeping, or tent-keeping, cook your own food, wash your own clothes, and sort your own gear, no one else is going to. Your mother won't be around and the elves will be distracted by other outdoor diversions.

—Christopher Wren

Nick slipped off his pack and lay down in the shade. He lay on his back and looked up into the pine trees. His neck and back and the small of his back rested as he stretched. The earth felt good against his back. He looked up at the sky, through the branches, and then shut his eyes. He opened them and looked up again. There was a wind high up in the branches. He shut his eyes again and went to sleep.

—Ernest Hemingway

If you are looking down while you are walking it is better to walk up hill the ground is nearer.

—Gertrude Stein

The pay is good and I can walk to work.

—John F. Kennedy, on the presidency

The westerner, normally, walks to get somewhere that he cannot get in an automobile or on horseback. Hiking for its own sake, for the sheer animal pleasure of good condition and brisk exercise, is not an easy thing for him to comprehend.

—*The WPA Guide to Utah*, 1941

My Other Car Is a Pair of Boots

—Bumper sticker

Keep your eyes on the stars, but remember to keep your feet on the ground.

—Theodore Roosevelt

The wisdom of age: don't stop walking.

—Mason Cooley

solitude and companionship

Is it better to tread ground in good company, or all alone? Each option has its benefits and its drawbacks—and passionate proponents, too.

When I dance, I dance; when I sleep, I sleep; yes, and when I walk alone in a beautiful orchard, if my thoughts have been dwelling elsewhere, I bring them back to the walk, to the orchard, to the sweetness of this solitude, and to me.

—Michel de Montaigne

Here's to the day when it is May
And care as light as a feather,
When your little shoes and my big boots
Go tramping over the heather.

—Bliss Carman

Still, I search in these woods and find nothing worse
than myself, caught between the grapes and the thorns.

—Anne Sexton

Take nothing for granted. Not one blessed, cool mountain day or one hellish, desert day or one sweaty, stinky hiking companion. It is all a gift.

—Cindy Ross

For the first time, I would be alone since beginning my hike. With that thought, I was happy and lonely at the same time.

—Jeff Alt

Weekend planning is a prime time to apply the Deathbed Priority Test: On your deathbed, will you wish you'd spent more prime weekend hours grocery shopping or walking in the woods with your kids?

—Louise Lague

Think me not unkind and rude
That I walk alone in grove and glen;
I go to the god of the wood
To fetch his word to men.

—Ralph Waldo Emerson

I still find each day too short for all the thoughts I want to think, all the walks I want to take, all the books I want to read, and all the friends I want to see.

—John Burroughs

Though the most beautiful creature were waiting for me at the end of a journey or a walk; though the carpet were of silk, the curtains of the morning clouds; the chairs and sofa stuffed with cygnet's down; the food manna, the wine beyond claret, the window opening on Winandermere, I should not feel—or rather my happiness would not be so fine, as my solitude is sublime.

—John Keats

I hope we shall each be the happier in the others' company. And, Gentlemen, that I may not lose yours, I shall either abate or amend my pace to enjoy it, knowing that, as the Italians say, "Good company in a journey makes the way to seem the shorter."

—Izaak Walton

O sweet woods, the delight of solitariness!

—Sir Philip Sidney

Possibly it is not lonesome to walk alone through the woods or the crowded city streets because in the woods one has nature to commune with, and in the city there are so many sights to see. And yet walking alone in the forest would be too much like the life of Robinson Crusoe before Friday turned up to bring him problems and to bring him fellowship. I think we all want our Fridays even when we are not on a desert island.

—Grace Hastings Sharp

I needed to go solo. I wanted to test myself to see how far I could go, how well I could hike without the worries of making sure someone else was sufficiently entertained and content.

—Lisa Marie Pane

When I go camping in the Green Mountains, it is most likely to be with our entire family. When I go out on hikes by myself, I almost always come home at night to prepare and eat a meal with Rita and our children and to sleep in our own bed with my wife. All of us in the family take our individual outings in the nearby woods. But the shared points of reference ... are so familiar that when we share our individual stories they naturally intertwine into a collective web ...

—John Elder

I don't like to be idle; in fact, I often feel somewhat guilty unless there is some purpose to what I am doing. But spending a few hours—or a few days—in the woods, swamps, or alongside a stream has never seemed to me a waste of time … I derive special benefit from a period of solitude.

—Jimmy Carter

I encountered long periods of perfect aloneness, when I didn't see another soul for hours; many times when I would wait for Katz for a long spell and no other hiker would come along. When that happened, I would leave my pack and go back and find him, to see that he was all right, which always pleased him. Sometimes he would be proudly bearing my stick, which I had left by a tree when I had stopped to tie my laces or adjust my pack. We seemed to be looking out for each other.

—Bill Bryson

One of the pleasantest things in the world is going on a journey; but I like to go by myself. I can enjoy society in a room; but out of doors, nature is company enough for me.

—William Hazlitt

I like long walks, especially when they are taken by people who annoy me.

—Fred Allen

Always in big woods when you leave familiar ground and step off alone into a new place there will be, along with the feelings of curiosity and excitement, a little nagging of dread … You are undertaking the first experience, not of the place, but of yourself in that place. It is an experience of our essential loneliness, for nobody can discover the world for anybody else. It is only after we have discovered it for ourselves that it becomes a common ground and a common bond, and we cease to be alone.

—Wendell Berry

Curious children are great hiking companions; their vitality and exuberance lend an energy to the experience that cannot be duplicated.

—Bryan MacKay

I find it wholesome to be alone the greater part of the time. To be in company, even with the best, is soon wearisome and dissipating. I love to be alone. I never found the companion that was so companionable as solitude.

—Henry David Thoreau

He sits and thinks of the things they know,
He and the Forest, alone together ...

—A. A. Milne

I wish I could walk for a day and a night,
And find me at dawn in a desolate place
With never the rut of a road in sight,
Or the roof of a house, or the eyes of a face.

—Edna St. Vincent Millay

The woods were mine. I tried to persuade friends to accompany me, and sometimes they would, but they saw little point to my wanderings … With an apple and a piece of cheese or bread in my pocket, I would go out as soon as I had finished my daily chores and walk six miles, eight miles, ten miles, returning only for supper. Walking alone was a fierce high joy. I didn't have to explain or justify myself.

—Marge Piercy

How I long to be away, down there in the country, at my father's house, out in the fields at night, walking alone, all, all alone! Ah, good it is in the country at night walking with a stick, forward and forward, on and on, dreaming all sorts of things; silently, in the vast lonely countryside, swinging along the deep roads; ah good it is, good!

—Edouard Dujardin

walking for body, mind, and spirit

At the end of the day, walking may be the one sure way to clear the head, break a sweat, and travel toward enlightenment, all at once. Not bad for a simple activity.

Men go out to admire the heights of mountains, the huge waves of the sea, the broadest spans of rivers, the circle of ocean, the revolutions of stars, and leave themselves behind.

—St. Augustine

Walking has been one of the constellations in the starry sky of human culture, a constellation whose three stars are the body, the imagination, and the wide-open world, and though all three exist independently, it is the lines drawn between them—drawn by the act of walking for cultural purposes—that makes them a constellation.

—Rebecca Solnit

In my room, the world is beyond my understanding;
But when I walk I see that it consists of three or four
Hills and a cloud.

—Wallace Stevens

Walking is the very best exercise. Habituate yourself to
walk very far.

—Thomas Jefferson

After you eat always take a walk, and you'll never have to go to a medicine shop.

—Chinese proverb

Every day I walk myself into a state of well-being and walk away from every illness; I have walked myself into my best thoughts, and I know of no thought so burdensome that one cannot walk away from it.

—Søren Kierkegaard

I love going for walks. My father is a great walker—
he does a lot of it. But it's quite nice because you can just
go off and ponder. You can think about things. It's your
own time.

—Prince William

And as you sit on the hillside, or lie prone under the trees of the forest, or sprawl wet-legged on the shingly beach of a mountain stream, the great door, that does not look like a door, opens.

—Stephen Graham

It's strange how deserts turn us into believers. I believe in walking in a landscape of mirages, because you learn humility. I believe in living in a land of little water because life is drawn together. And I believe in the gathering of bones as a testament to spirits that have moved on.

—Terry Tempest Williams

May your trails be crooked, winding, lonesome, dangerous, leading to the most amazing view. May your mountains rise into and above the clouds. May your rivers flow without end, meandering through pastoral valleys tinkling with bells, past temples and castles and poets' towers into a dark primeval forest where tigers belch and monkeys howl, through miasmal and mysterious swamps and down into a desert of red rock, blue mesas, domes and pinnacles and grottos of endless stone, and down again into a deep vast ancient unknown chasm where bars of sunlight blaze on profiled cliffs, where deer walk across the white sand beaches, where storms come and go as lightning clangs upon the high crags, where something strange and more beautiful and more full of wonder than your deepest dreams waits for you—beyond that next turning of the canyon walls.

—Edward Abbey

People usually consider walking on water or in thin air a miracle. But I think the real miracle is not to walk either on water or in thin air, but to walk on earth. Every day we are engaged in a miracle which we don't even recognize: a blue sky, white clouds, green leaves, the black, curious eyes of a child—our own two eyes. All is a miracle.

—Thich Nhat Hanh

Walk in Balance.

—Meditative saying

Why are there trees I never walk under but large and melodious thoughts descend upon me?

—Walt Whitman

After more than two thousand miles on the [Appalachian] trail, you can expect to undergo some personality changes. A heightened affinity for nature infiltrates your life. Greater inner peace. Enhanced self-esteem. A quiet confidence that if I could do that, I can do and should do whatever I really want to do … A renewed faith in the essential goodness of humankind. And a determination to repay others for the many kindnesses you have received.

—Larry Luxenberg

Walking makes for a long life.

—Hindu proverb

[Walking] does more than push a little blood through my broken-down arteries. Walking makes me feel more alive, more aware of the world around me. It awakens my senses, improves my outlook on life. It helps me see.

—John P. Wiley Jr.

My grandfather, for instance, lived to be a well-adjusted 95 … by walking a few brisk miles every morning and avoiding between-meal snacks.

—Bill McKibben

Walking is a very good method of meditation. You simply stroll around, but be right with it! Be *here*.

—Alan Watts

Walking is nearly as natural as breathing. Most of us don't remember learning how—it's just something that happens. And when it does—one foot in front of the other, one foot in front of the other—thoughts are free to go skipping over the landscape like thistledown on the wind.

—Cathy Johnson

I'm happy when I'm hiking, pack upon my back.
I'm happy when I'm hiking, off the beaten track.

—English hiking song

[The] world cannot be discovered by a journey of miles, no matter how long, but only by a spiritual journey, a journey of one inch, very arduous and humbling and joyful, by which we arrive at the ground at our feet, and learn to be at home. It is a journey we can make only by the acceptance of mystery and mystification—by yielding to the condition that what we have expected is not there.

—Wendell Berry

Give me the clear blue sky over my head, and the green turf beneath my feet, a winding road before me, and a three hours' march to dinner—and then to thinking!

—William Hazlitt

All the ways that lead to Somewhere
Echo with the hurrying feet
Of the Struggling and the Striving,
But the way I find so sweet
Bids me dream and bids me linger,
Joy and Beauty are its goal,—
On the path that leads to Nowhere
I have sometimes found my soul!

—Corinne Roosevelt Robinson

I feel as though I found Zen while walking in the woods … A pebble thrown into a pond creates ripples of water which send ripples into the air and so on and so forth … This rippling effect followed me back into society and strengthened my beliefs in the interconnectedness of all things. It boosted my beliefs that people must be good to each other, as the ripples aren't just in the water, but in the conversations we have with others as well.

—Sam Haraldson

I only went out for a walk, and finally concluded to stay out till sundown, for going out, I found, was really going in.

—John Muir